Around and Through

Luana Mitten and Meg Greve

ROURKE PUBLISHING

Vero Beach, Florida 32964

www.rourkepublishing.com

PHOTO CREDITS: © Nicole S. Young: 3; © fred hall: 4, 5; © Cameron Whitman: 8, 9; © Marilyn Nieves: 10, 11; © creatingmore: 13; © kihoto: 14, 15; © Scott Williams: 16, 17; © Ina Peters: 18, 19; © David Stevenson: 20; © iofoto: 21; © Tyson Paul: 22, 23

Editor: Luana Mitten

Cover design by Nicola Stratford, bdpublishing.com

Interior Design by Tara Raymo

DEC 07 '09

Library of Congress Cataloging-in-Publication Data

Mitten, Luana K.
 Around and through / Luana Mitten and Meg Greve.
   p. cm. -- (Concepts)
 Includes bibliographical references and index.
 ISBN 978-1-60694-385-4 (alk. paper) (hardcover)
 ISBN 978-1-60694-517-9 (softcover)
 ISBN 978-1-60694-575-9 (bilingual)
1. Space perception--Juvenile literature. I. Greve, Meg. II. Title.
 BF469.K578 2010
 423'.12--dc22

                          2009016026

Printed in the USA

CG/CG

www.rourkepublishing.com - rourke@rourkepublishing.com
Post Office Box 643328 Vero Beach, Florida 32964

Around or through?
Around or through?
I want to play at the
park with you!

3

Should I go around, or should I go through?

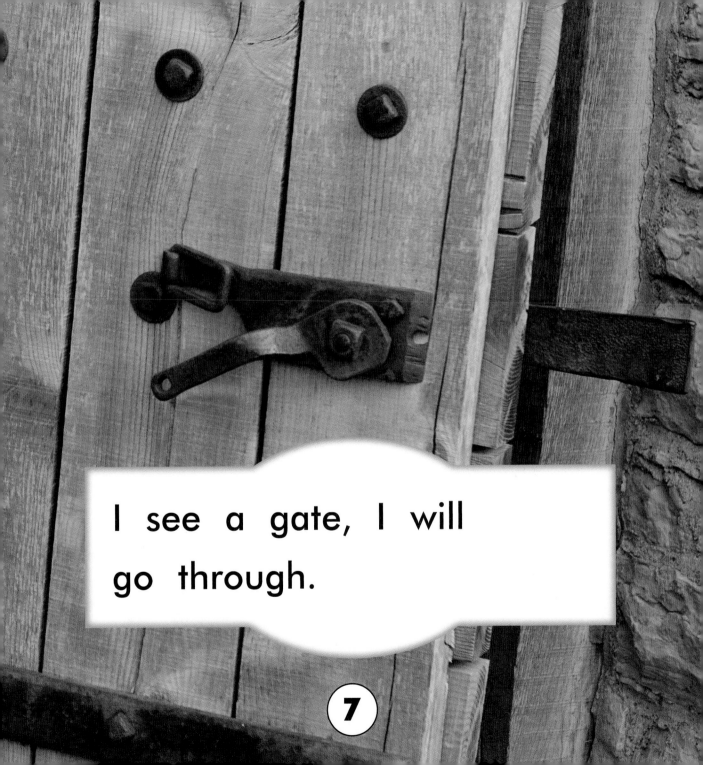

I see a gate, I will go through.

Should I go around, or should I go through?

I run around the pole,
not through!

11

Should I go around, or should I go through?

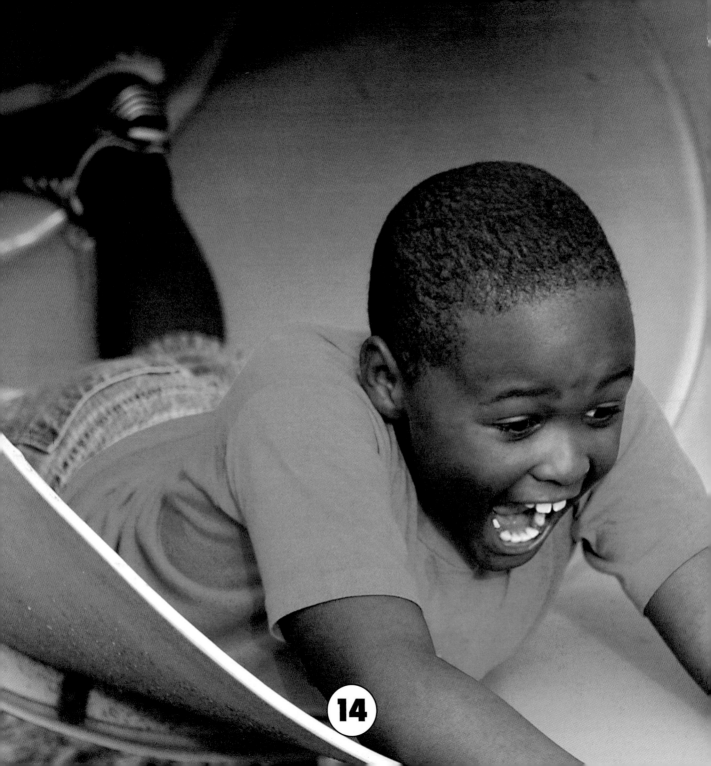

I see a tunnel, I will go through!

Should I go around, or should I go through?

I will go around the swings, not through!

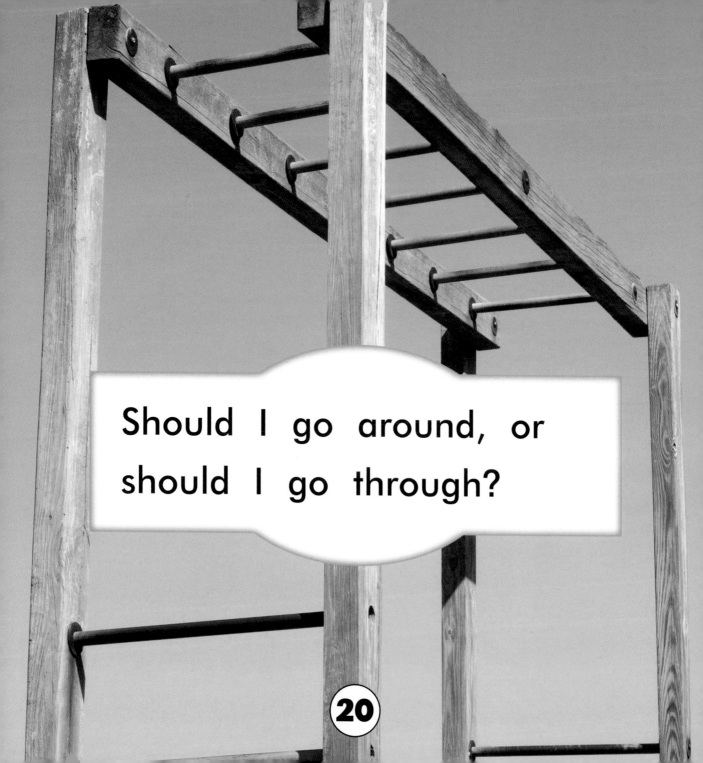

Should I go around, or
should I go through?

I see monkey bars. I will go around AND through!

21

1, 2, 3, look and see.

What do you go around and what do you go through?

23

Index

Websites to Visit

urbanext.illinois.edu/hopping/rhymes.html

www.funbrain.com/brain/SweepsBrain/sweepsbrain.html

pbskids.org/arthur/games/poetry/poems/350440.html

About the Authors

Thanks to phone calls and e-mails, Meg Greve and Luana Mitten can work together even though they live about 1,200 miles (1,900 kilometers) apart. Meg lives in the big city of Chicago, Illinois and gets to play in the snow with her kids. Luana lives on a golf course in Tampa, Florida and gets freckles on her face from playing at the beach with her son.

Artist: Madison Greve